COLOR MY INSPIRATIONS
Vol I

Mandalas for Fun and Relaxation

by Dottie Cooper Katz

www.cooperk.com

All content of this book is the sole property of the artist and in no way may be used in whole or in part without permission. The images in this book may be printed for the purpose of coloring for personal use only. Once you have purchased this book you may print the coloring pages as many times as you like for coloring. If you post on social media, please put a couple pencils on the page to show this is not a freebie for others to color. These images took time and effort to create for your enjoyment. Thank you.

ISBN-13:
978-1519415806

ISBN-10:
151941580X

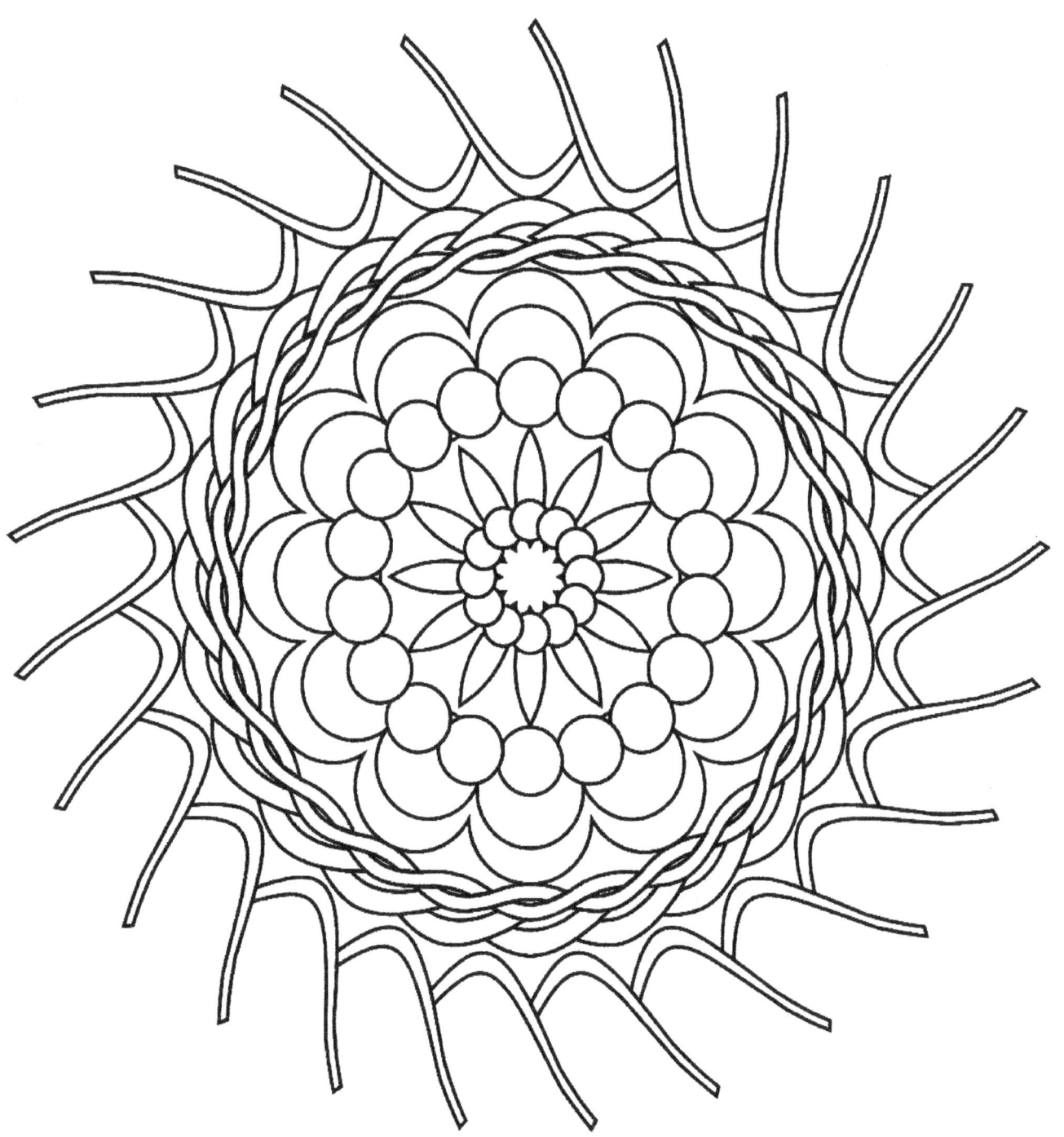

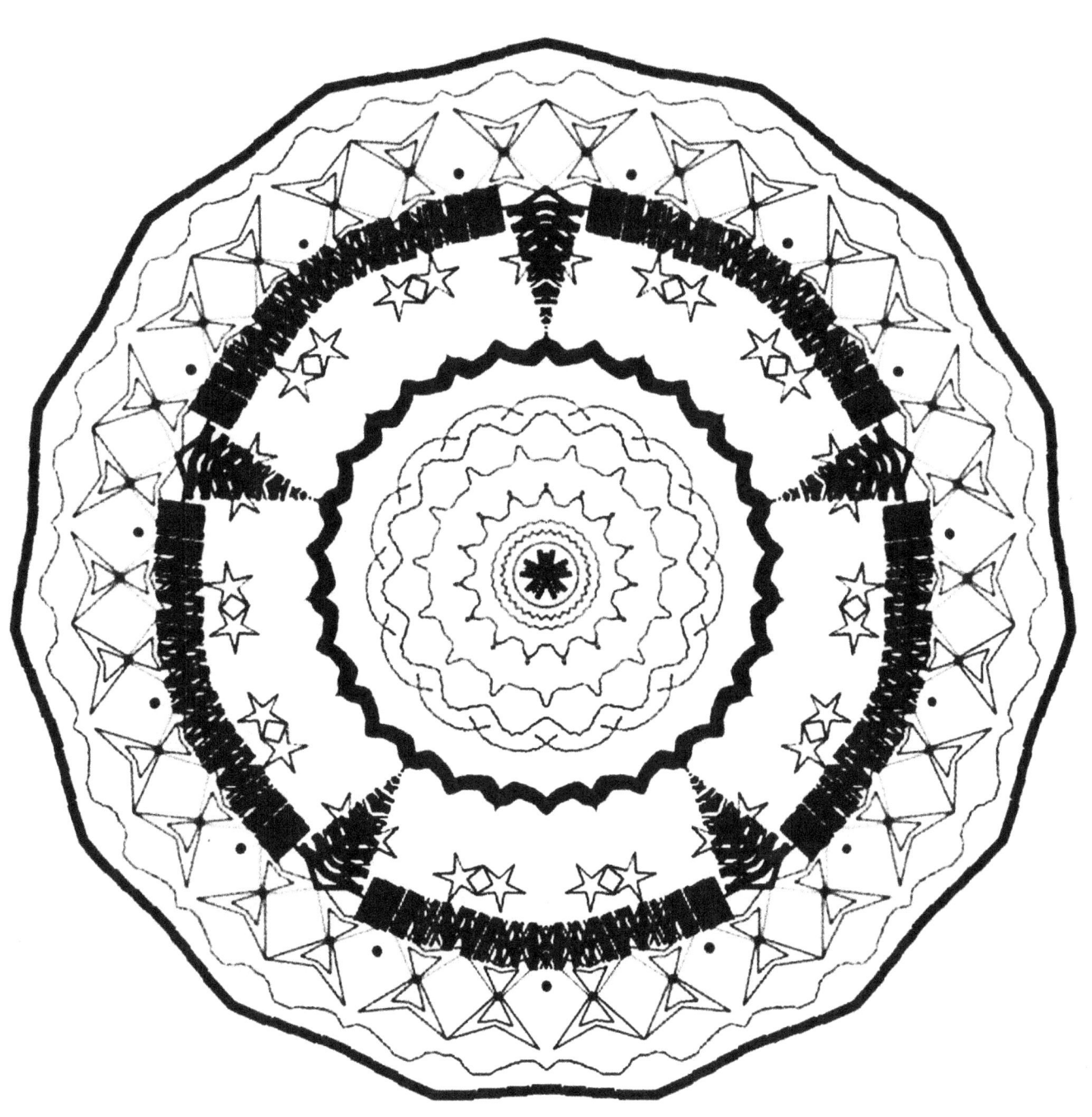

Dedicated to the adult lovers of coloring. It has brought me renewed inspiration for drawing. I enjoy creating with designs that come from all over the world and am looking forward to seeing how you color them.

Thank you all.

Dottie